Ancient Civilizations

The forests of Quebec (kwih•BEK), a region in what is known today as Canada, stretch for hundreds of miles. Long ago, the trees went from one end of Quebec to the other without a break. Even today most of Quebec is untouched wilderness.

The first people who lived in Quebec had a story about those trees. The story has been passed down through the centuries, and here's what it says: In the ancient days, there was a god named Gluskap who had made humans and other animals. One day, four people came to Gluskap. Each had a wish. The first person wanted to be nicer. The second person wanted a home. The third person wanted people to stop laughing at him. And the fourth person was a man who wanted to be taller and more handsome than any other man around.

Gluskap granted their wishes. The first three people got exactly what they asked for. The fourth person did become taller and more handsome than anyone else. He grew and grew and spread his arms. He became the first and the biggest of the pine trees that cover Quebec.

That story comes from the Algonquians (al•GAHN•kee•uhnz). They were a group of Native American tribes who lived in Quebec long before the Europeans arrived. Although there were many different tribes of Algonquians, they all spoke a similar language. The way they lived and dressed was also similar. Some Algonquians lived in what is now the United States. Many Algonquian tribes still live in New England and also in Canada.

Algonquians lived in wigwams, which have a frame of poles made of small trees. The poles are covered with animal skins or tree bark. Near the bottom is an opening covered by a flaplike door. The very top of the wigwam has an opening, too, so that smoke from fires can escape. Wigwams can be taken apart easily, which was handy for the Algonquians because they liked to move. Every few months they would pack up their camp and go to a new site.

The Algonquians hunted wild game such as deer. They also fished, and they gathered berries and seeds from the forest. They moved according to the seasons, hunting and gathering different foods at different times of the year. They walked or traveled by water in sturdy canoes. In winter when the rivers were frozen, they traveled using snowshoes or sleds.

Algonquians could quickly build and take apart their wigwams.

Other Native Americans lived in Quebec, too. One important group was the Iroquois (ihr•uh•KWOY). They included five different nations, or tribes. They were farmers who raised corn, beans, and squash. Because they wanted to stay close to their fields, they lived in villages year-round. The villages were made up of buildings called *longhouses*. One longhouse might be 200 feet (61 m) in length. That's more than half the length of a football field.

Longhouses had rounded roofs covered in tree bark. Inside, rows of wooden ledges were built along the walls. These ledges were like bunk beds. People slept on them and stored things underneath.

An average of ten families lived in each longhouse. At night the families would gather around their fires to eat and tell stories. The fires burned in a row down the middle of the longhouse. Corn from the harvest was hung high on the walls, and it glistened like gold in the light.

The Iroquois put a lot of work into building their longhouses and tending their fields. They did not want all this effort to go to waste. That's partly why they came together to form one nation. They wanted to better defend themselves against the Algonquians and other tribes.

An Iroquois longhouse.

The Native American tribes often fought one another. They fought over the right to live or hunt in certain places. But they did not believe that they owned the land. This was a very different view from that of the Europeans. During the 1500s explorers from Europe began arriving in the New World. They claimed vast lands for their countries.

The Iroquois harvested corn, or maize, as did many Native American tribes.

The French Arrive

French explorer Jacques Cartier (ZHAHK kar•TYAY) arrived in Quebec in 1534. He and other members of his expedition had crossed the Atlantic Ocean with two small ships. The voyage took three weeks. Although it was May, large chunks of ice still floated in the chilly waters. Cartier wasn't thrilled by the weather, but he did love the scenery. He saw thousands of birds that "skim as quickly through the water as other birds do through the air."

Cartier also saw Native Americans for the first time. No one is certain of the tribe's name, but here's how he described them:

They wore their hair "tied up on top of their heads like a handful of twisted hay, with a nail or something of the sort passed through the middle . . . into which they weave a few bird's feathers."

Jacques Cartier discovered the St. Lawrence River and the site that later became Quebec City.

In the early days of Quebec, fur trading was a vital part of the economy.

Cartier anchored near the Gaspé Peninsula. There he made his first real contact with Native Americans. Members of the Micmac tribe approached in canoes. A nervous Cartier fired a cannonball over their heads. The Micmacs returned the next day with animal furs as peace offerings. Cartier gave them knives, bells, and combs in trade. This friendly exchange marked the beginning of the fur trade that would thrive in Quebec for years.

Days later Cartier met the Iroquois. Their heads were almost completely shaved except for the long ponytails that trailed down their backs. The Iroquois exchanged gifts with the Europeans. But when Cartier stuck a wooden cross in the ground to claim the land for France, the Native Americans were angered. The Iroquois now understood that these strange-looking Frenchmen in their big boats wanted to take over the land.

When Cartier returned to Europe from his second trip to Quebec, he took with him a group of Iroquois, including a chief. He promised to return them safely, but they died in France. When Cartier returned to Quebec six years later to establish a settlement, the Iroquois were angry with him. They began raiding the French settlement. In 1543 the French gave up and sailed for home. Sixty years would pass before the next French explorer appeared in Quebec.

In 1603 an explorer named Samuel de Champlain (sham•PLAYN) achieved what Cartier could not. Champlain founded a lasting French settlement, at Quebec City. He did this in part by making friends with the Algonquians. He even fought on the side of the Algonquians against their enemy, the Iroquois. This made the Algonquians strong allies of the French. Of course, it gave the Iroquois one more reason to dislike the French.

Samuel de Champlain established a lasting French settlement in 1603.

Soon other settlements were founded, including Montreal and Trois-Rivières (twah ree•VYAIR). The settlers were mainly soldiers, hired workers, and missionaries. Very few women immigrated to the new land. During the early 1600s most Europeans thought of the colony, known as New France, as a cold, wild place with hungry bears. The voyage across the Atlantic was not easy, either. Eventually, however, the settlements grew.

Champlain, the founder of the first French settlement in Quebec, remains a mystery. Little is known about his early life. Historians are not even certain of his date of birth. They do know that he died in Quebec City in 1635. There was even a mystery surrounding his death. To this day no one knows where he is buried. People in Quebec still search for the grave of their city's founder.

Samuel de Champlain's map shows New France in 1632.

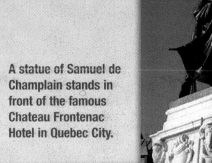

A statue of Samuel de Champlain stands in front of the famous Chateau Frontenac Hotel in Quebec City.

The Country Changes Hands

James Wolfe led his army against French troops on the Plains of Abraham.

View of the Taking of QUEBECK by the Engl...

The colony of New France grew rich from the fur trade.
Beaver and other furs were in great demand in Europe.
France's longtime rival, England, had made friends with
the Iroquois. The Iroquois still did not like the French at all.

RIVER St. LAWRENCE

QUE BE CK

rces Commanded by Gen.ˡ Wolfe Sep: 13.ᵗʰ 175

War broke out in Europe between these two powers, the French and the English. The conflict spread to the colonies in 1754. British colonists and their allies, the Iroquois, fought the French colonists and their Algonquian allies. In the United States this war is called the French and Indian War.

The two sides were far from evenly matched. France had 5,000 soldiers in North America. England had more than 23,000. Still, both armies won victories, and the war swung back and forth. Then in the summer of 1759, the English general, James Wolfe, sailed with his fleet toward Quebec City. This city, the heart of New France, was built on high ground and protected by rugged cliffs. Wolfe camped his soldiers within sight of the city. The French commander, the Marquis de Montcalm, camped his army behind the city walls.

For almost 3 months the two armies engaged in scattered fighting. Cannonballs launched from the English camp reduced the city to ruins. But Montcalm avoided all-out warfare. Winter came early to Quebec, and he was hoping that the cold weather would force the English to retreat.

Wolfe, however, declared, "I will have Quebec if I stay here till the end of November." He came up with a bold plan. First, he put his soldiers back on their ships. Then, in the dead of night, he sailed past the French camp. The British climbed a narrow path to the top of the cliffs. When the French awoke, the English army was lined up before them on a stretch of land called the Plains of Abraham.

On that day, September 13, the two armies met in final battle. Wolfe himself led the charge and was shot three times before finally dying. Montcalm was also wounded just hours before Quebec fell. His last words before he died of his wounds were, "I am happy that I shall not live to see the surrender of Quebec."

The battle on the Plains of Abraham marked the beginning of the end of the French and Indian War. France gave up most of its lands in North America. Quebec now belonged to England. But in their hearts, the people were still proudly French.

James Wolfe died after his victory over the French in Quebec.

Out From Under
England's
Thumb

The following years were hard on the French people of Quebec. They were under the rule of their longtime enemy, England. English was now the official language in government and in schools. The government leaders were all English. None had been elected to office. They were all appointed by England. The French were resentful.

The situation grew worse after the American Revolution. Some American colonists had supported the English. When the British were defeated, loyal colonists fled to the British colonies in Canada. Thousands moved to Quebec. The French people of Quebec and the new English colonists did not get along.

England decided to split up the two groups. In 1791 Canada was divided in two. Lower Canada, the home of most of the French people, was the area we now call Quebec. Upper Canada, settled mainly by English people, included the province now known as Ontario.

At the same time, the fur trade crashed. In 1770 it made up more than 75 percent of Quebec's exports. That number had fallen to 9 percent by 1810. Most former fur traders were French. They were forced into poverty.

Things continued to get worse for the French-speaking people. Encouraged by England, one million immigrants came to Canada between 1800 and 1850. French colonists were threatened by these people who would make jobs, food, and places to live more scarce. Many of the immigrants were crowded into ships with little food and water. When the immigrants came ashore, they brought with them a terrible disease called cholera, which quickly spread through the city. Quebec was struck by two cholera epidemics, one in 1832 and another just two years later. Thousands died.

European immigrants arrive in Canada.

A highlight of the winter carnival in Quebec City is the Ice Palace, which is built with tons of ice.

Then in 1867, the nation of Canada was formed. It included Quebec, Ontario, New Brunswick, and Nova Scotia. For the people of Quebec, this was a step forward. They were given the right to speak French, to make laws in French, and to teach French to their children. Modern Quebec was born.

Quebec has gone through many changes since then. Its cities have grown as people have traded farming and fur trapping for jobs in industry and business. In 1861 roughly 15 percent of the population lived in cities. By 1901 that number had jumped to nearly 40 percent.

Quebec City has grown. Around the old city are many new neighborhoods. The walls of the old city still stand above the Plains of Abraham. The walls and the narrow streets inside make it feel like an old European city.

Every winter, about a million visitors flock to Quebec City for the annual winter carnival. There's an ice-sculpting contest, fireworks, a parade, and canoe races across the frozen St. Lawrence River. The festival lasts for ten days.

Montreal expanded from a small missionary settlement to the second-largest French-speaking city in the world. Today it is called the Paris of the North. Located on the St. Lawrence Seaway, it's also the world's largest inland port. The city hosted the Expo '67 World's Fair and the 1976 Summer Olympics. It also has a major league baseball team, the Montreal Expos.

Under its bustling streets lies Montreal's famed "underground city," which features more than 18 miles (29 m) of walkways and passageways. These walkways connect hotels, movie theaters, stores, restaurants, and concert halls. They make it easier to get around during the cold winters.

BIGGER Than Texas

Quebec is 524,251 square miles (1,357,811 sq km) and is the largest province of Canada. The state of Texas is about half the size of Quebec.

RUE NOTRE-DAME OUEST

Notre-Dame is one of many historic buildings in Old Montreal.

Pour hot maple syrup on snow and you get maple taffy.

Snowmobiling is a popular activity in Quebec during the winter.

Wild About Quebec

Most of Quebec's population now lives in or near cities. Yet even today more than 75 percent of Quebec is still untouched wilderness. The province is still covered by thick forests and sparkling lakes. Much of the land is preserved in some 35 parks and wildlife refuges. One of the largest parks, the La Verendrye Reserve (la vair•AHN•dray REZ•air•vay), has more than 4,000 lakes and rivers!

The people of Quebec love activities in the great outdoors. One favorite pastime is snowmobiling. The first snowmobile was actually invented by a citizen of Quebec, Joseph-Armand Bombardier, in 1922. Today more than 18,600 miles (29,932 km) of snowmobile trails cross the province. The trails even have lodges and refueling stops for long-distance travel.

Many people use their snowmobiles to engage in another favorite sport, ice-fishing. During winter small "towns" of ice-fishing shacks dot the frozen surfaces of Quebec's lakes and rivers. Quebec is also famous for its skiing—it gets an average of 10 feet (3 m) of snow each year and has more than 800 ski trails.

Winter's not the only season for outdoor fun in Quebec. Summer brings sea-kayaking, white-water rafting, and rock climbing. A day at the shore might be spent watching whales. Ten species of whales migrate past the Quebec coast each summer. In the fall, the great forests that cover more than half of the province blaze in purple, red, and gold. It's a good time for hiking or biking, or enjoying a crisp apple from an orchard.

Spring brings a special treat—maple syrup. Quebec has more than 400 maple sugar companies. When the days start to grow longer, the maple farmers head to the forest with their buckets. They tap into the trunks of maple trees and collect the sap in the buckets. Then it's back to the "sugar shack" to boil the sap into thick, sweet syrup. Every spring, people flock to the sugar shacks to feast on traditional dishes. There's ham glazed with syrup, maple sugar pie, dumplings in maple syrup, and maple pudding.

Independence or No

Life for the people of Quebec has improved greatly since the province was founded. Pride in Quebec's French heritage has grown even stronger. Many people in Quebec believe the province should be a separate country. This is known as *separatism*.

In 1967 the president of France, Charles de Gaulle, visited Montreal. He shouted to his audience, "Vive le Quebec libre!" (veev leh kay•BEK LEEB•reh). To this cry of "Long live free Quebec!" the crowd wildly cheered. This event encouraged even more separatist feeling.

One year after de Gaulle's visit, Pierre Elliott Trudeau became prime minister of Canada. He was the second person from Quebec to hold this office. During his term French was made the second language of Canada. Government workers had to learn both French and English. Road signs gave directions in both languages. Trudeau did these things to keep Canada united. He felt that if the whole country paid more attention to French culture, the people of Quebec would be satisfied and stay part of Canada.

The separatist Parti Quebecois was elected to lead the province in 1976. Four years later the issue of independence was put to a vote. Should Quebec split from Canada? About 60 percent of the people voted no.

In the meantime Canada was breaking its last colonial ties. Although it had been an independent nation since 1867, it was still officially part of the British empire. A new Canadian constitution was adopted in 1982. Quebec, however, did not sign the constitution. It wanted the Canadian government to do more to preserve French cultures.

The tug-of-war continued into the next decade. In 1995 Quebec held a second vote on the issue of separatism. It was breathtakingly close: 50.6 percent of the people voted to remain with Canada; 49.4 percent voted to split. Once again, Quebec stayed part of Canada.

Much has changed in Quebec over the years, but much remains the same. Quebec is still a land of great beauty. The trees about which the Algonquians told stories still stand. But the cities of Montreal and Quebec are booming. French culture and traditions are stronger than ever. The province has ever-growing ties to the rest of Canada and to the world. In the years to come, who knows what new changes will take place?

Traffic signs in Quebec are in both French and English.

Quebec at night.

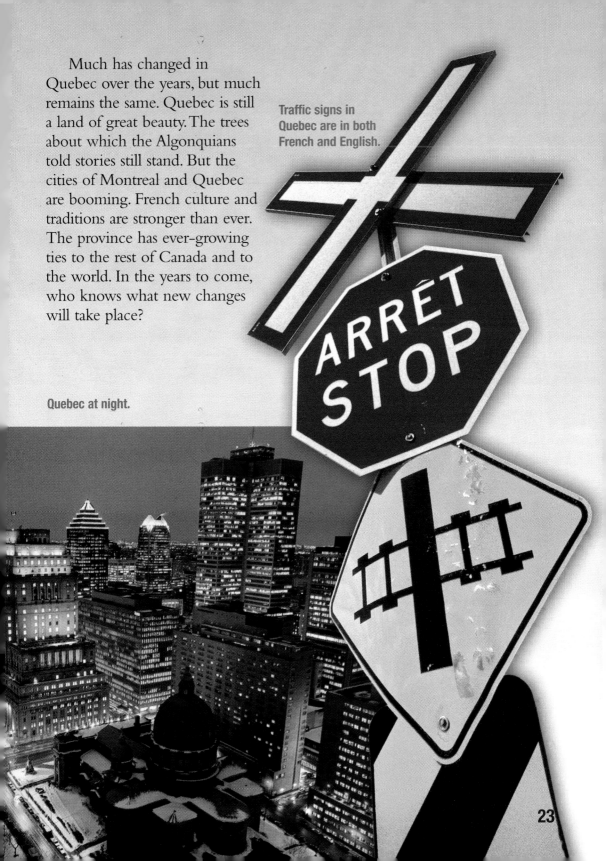

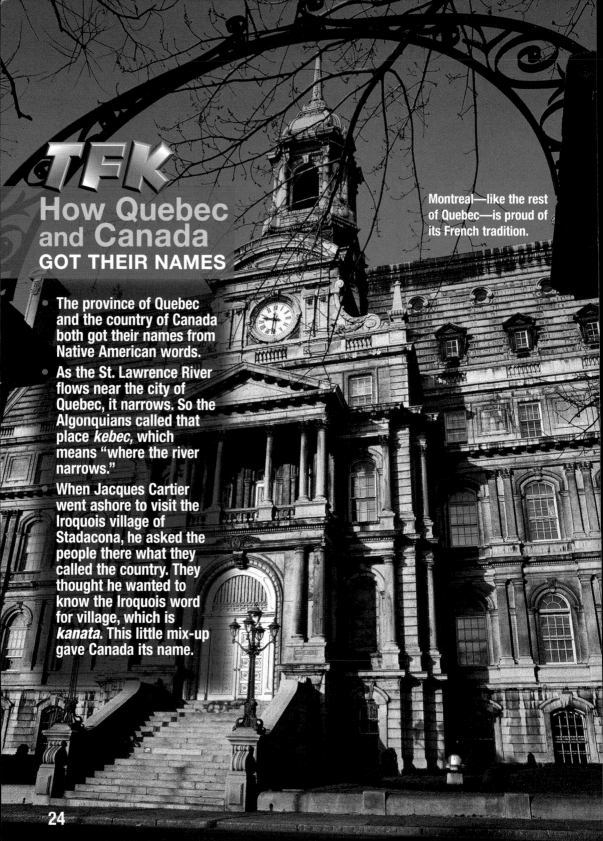

TFK

How Quebec and Canada
GOT THEIR NAMES

Montreal—like the rest of Quebec—is proud of its French tradition.

- The province of Quebec and the country of Canada both got their names from Native American words.

- As the St. Lawrence River flows near the city of Quebec, it narrows. So the Algonquians called that place *kebec*, which means "where the river narrows."

When Jacques Cartier went ashore to visit the Iroquois village of Stadacona, he asked the people there what they called the country. They thought he wanted to know the Iroquois word for village, which is *kanata*. This little mix-up gave Canada its name.